TO BE

remembered

your thoughts deserve
a decent place
to live

also by R. Clift

evolved poetry series
TO FEEL ANYTHING AT ALL

UNTIL WE MEET AGAIN
YOUR THOUGHTS DESERVE A DECENT PLACE TO LIVE

TO BE

REMEMBERED

for my mother

WITHOUT YOU, I WOULD HAVE NEVER KNOWN
HOW MUCH COURAGE IT TAKES
TO KEEP MOVING FORWARD.

WHAT IS AN EVOLVED POEM?

Photography is how I see the world,
poetry is how I interpret it.
I wished to meld my two passions together–
so this project was born.

For this autumn series, I chose a handful of poems,
two dear friends, and took them to secluded locations in
nature to explore and shoot.
In short, we read the poems one by one, pinpointed the
feeling from the words and found a way
to recreate that feeling visually in a photograph.

These photos are essentially, themselves, poems.

I'd like to thank the remarkable Emily and Ellen for
following me deep into forests, through winding dirt
trails, and across old railroad tracks all for the sake
of art, poetry, and human emotion.

xx –R

r.clift

GRIEF HELD MY HAND
WHEN YOU LEFT

GRIEF WAS THERE IN THE MIDDLE OF THE NIGHT
AFTER EVERYONE ELSE HAD GONE HOME

OUT OF RAGE AND EXHAUSTION I BLAMED IT
FOR THE PAIN I FELT

THE CONSTANT SORROW,
AGONY, LOSS, EMPTINESS

I DIDN'T REALIZE THIS WAS SOMETHING
I HAD TO GO THROUGH
i didn't realize grief was essential

AGAIN AND AGAIN I BLAMED MYSELF
FOR LOSING YOU. I BLAMED MY GRIEF
FOR KEEPING YOUR MEMORY SO CLOSE—

WHEN ALL IT WAS EVER TRYING TO DO
WAS HELP ME HEAL

STARS ARE MUCH LIKE HUMANS

THEY ARE BORN
THEY GROW OLD
and they die

SOME STARS FADE
SOME EXPLODE
BUT IN THE END
LIKE US

THEY ARE ONLY MORTAL

WE ARE ALL
BEAUTIFUL STORIES,
BUT THAT DOESN'T MEAN
OUR PAGES ARE
meant to be
IN THE SAME BOOK

MY MOTHER TAUGHT ME
MANY THINGS, BUT
SHE NEVER SHOWED ME
how to forget
ABOUT BEING IN LOVE
WITH SOMEONE WHO
LEFT

SO I JUST STUMBLE
AND FALL
INTO THE ARMS
OF ANOTHER

AND I FEAR
I WILL ALWAYS BE
TRAPPED IN THIS PLACE
OF LONGING FOR SOMEONE

WHO IS ALWAYS
JUST OUT OF REACH

IF I WERE TO FEEL
everything
AT THE INTENSITY
I AM CAPABLE OF—
I'D FALL APART

when was the last time
YOU LAUGHED WITHOUT GRIEF
HIDING IN THE CORNERS OF YOUR SMILE?

i still think of you
with every step i take

AS YOUR LOVE DID FOR ME,

SUMMER PASSED AWAY SLOWLY—

IT LAID DOWN SOFTLY,

stillness overtook

COLORS DIMMED

IT GREW COLD

SILENT

AND IN TIME

IT FADED AWAY TO NOTHING

AS IF IT HAD NEVER BEEN THERE AT ALL

WHILE I WAS VISITING MY GRANDPARENTS,
I HAPPENED TO NOTICE NEARBY,
A STRANGER'S TOMBSTONE
INSCRIBED WITH THE WORDS:

AS YOU ARE, I ONCE WAS
AS I AM, YOU SOON WILL BE

AND IF THAT DOESN'T
make a beating heart think twice
ABOUT TAKING EVEN A MOMENT
OF THIS LIFE
FOR GRANTED—
I DON'T KNOW WHAT WILL

r.clift

I THINK ONE OF THE HARDEST
THINGS ABOUT LOSING SOMEONE
IS SPEAKING OF THEM IN PAST TENSE—

HE WENT ON WALKS IN THE WOODS
HE GREW TOMATOES IN HIS GARDEN
HE TALKED QUIETLY
HE PUT CRACKERS IN HIS SOUP
HE READ THE FUNNIES FIRST
HE SAT IN THE BACK ROW OF AN OLD CHURCH
HE CARED FOR FLOWERS LIKE FRIENDS
HE LOVED ME

HE LOVED ME.

for my grandfather
1915 - 2017

I FEEL YOU QUICKLY

slipping away

LIKE THE OCEAN

THROUGH MY FINGERS

AND NOTHING I CAN DO

WILL SLOW IT DOWN

IMAGINE ALL THE HEARTS OUT THERE
that are broken
AND STILL
BEATING

YOU KNOW THAT LITTLE TUG
IN YOUR CHEST, THE ONE
THAT PULLS BACK AND FORTH
BETWEEN HAPPINESS AND
SADNESS WHEN YOU REMEMBER
SOMETHING
OR SOMEWHERE
OR SOMEONE YOU'VE LOST?

I USED TO HATE THAT FEELING, I
USED TO GET SO CAUGHT UP IN
WHAT WAS AND WHAT COULD NEVER BE AGAIN
THAT I COULDN'T APPRECIATE
THE HAPPENINGS OF NOW, OR UNDERSTAND
THAT THIS MOMENT WILL SOON
TUG AT MY HEART AS WELL

I HAVE LONG SINCE COME TO WELCOME
THAT TUG— BECAUSE EVEN THOUGH
it reminds me of what i have lost,
IT ALSO REMINDS ME OF
WHAT I WAS SO LUCKY TO LOVE

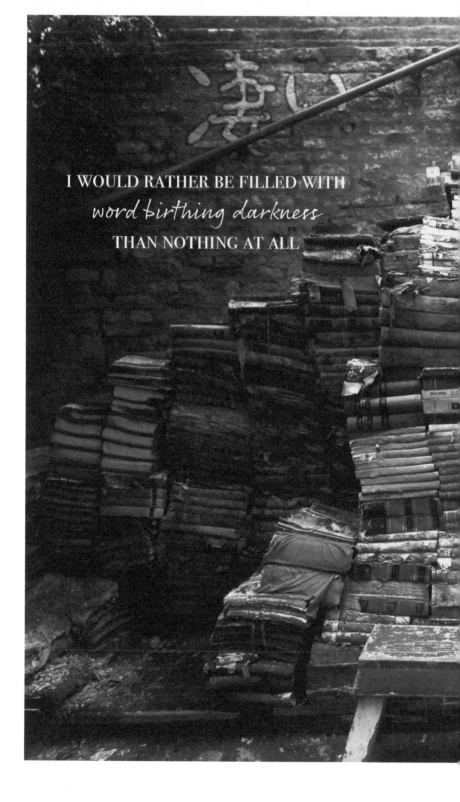

I WOULD RATHER BE FILLED WITH
word birthing darkness
THAN NOTHING AT ALL

i'm waiting for the day
YOU PLACE ME IN A BOX
AND SHOVE ME INTO THAT
DUSTY CORNER OF THE ATTIC,
LIKE AN OLD FAVORITE TOY
THAT WORE OUT

WHEN WILL YOU OUTGROW ME?
IT'S ONLY A MATTER OF TIME

SO PULL ME IN AND HOLD ME TIGHT
OR PUSH ME OUT AND SLAM THE DOOR
BECAUSE I'M TIRED OF TEETERING
on this threshold of wondering
IF I'M ALLOWED INSIDE YOUR HEART

THE ONLY THING I KNOW HOW TO DO,
with a heart like that
IS BREAK IT

YOU HAUNT ME LIKE THE
GHOST OF A LOVER. WHEN MY EYES CLOSE
I FEEL YOUR ARMS WRAP AROUND ME
IN THE BREEZE AND I HEAR YOUR VOICE
WHISPER MY NAME IN THE DARK

IT'S IN THE STILLNESS, WHEN
YOU'RE THERE, IN THE MOMENTS WHEN
I REMEMBER I'M ALONE.
SOMETIMES I'M A FOOL THINKING
IT COULD ACTUALLY BE YOU—
BUT IT IS ONLY EVER
THE WIND AND THE DARKNESS,
FOR WHEN I REACH OUT TO HOLD ON TO YOU
MY HANDS ALWAYS COME BACK EMPTY

I OPEN MY EYES AND YOU WERE NEVER
THERE. I SHOULD KNOW BY NOW YOU WILL
NEVER BE THERE. BUT STILL,
I KEEP REACHING—
AND MY HEART KEEPS
COMING BACK
EMPTY

MORE THAN ANYTHING I WISH
I COULD TELL YOU
HOW MUCH I MISS YOU—
BUT THAT IS ON THE LIST OF THINGS
i can never say again,
RIGHT BELOW I LOVE YOU

NO MATTER HOW MUCH
THIS BROKEN HEART HEALS
i still wake up alone

FOR THIS BRIEF MOMENT
LET HER FORGET

let her heart rest

LET HER EYES SPARKLE WITH
SOMETHING OTHER THAN TEARS

SHE TURNS UP THE MUSIC
AND CRANES HER NECK BACK
FOR ONE LAST GLIMPSE
OF A PLACE
SHE NEVER FULLY LEAVES BEHIND

AS IT GLIDES OUT OF SIGHT
SHE FEELS THE SAME DULL PAIN
AS HEARING THE WORDS
take care of yourself
FROM A VOICE SHE ONCE LOVED

AND WITHOUT
THE CITY LIGHTS TO GAZE AT
SHE MUST LOOK FORWARD
AND SETTLE FOR THE STARS

I'M ALONE

I'VE ALWAYS BEEN ALONE

I DON'T KNOW HOW TO BE

ANYTHING ELSE

i don't know how to feel

ANYTHING ELSE

I KNOW PEOPLE CAN CHANGE
BECAUSE I'VE
looked in the mirror
AND NOT RECOGNIZED
THE GIRL STARING BACK AT ME

I COME FROM A
CHARMINGLY LUCKLESS,
UNFORTUNATE PLACE
THAT IS TOO BIG TO BE A SMALL TOWN
AND TOO SMALL TO BE A BIG CITY

IT RESIDES SOMEWHERE BETWEEN
GRAVELY CLOSE
AND COMFORTABLY DISTANT—
WE ARE RAISED TO BLINDLY LOVE
AT AN ARM'S LENGTH AND
TO FEAR ANGELIC STRANGERS
MORE THAN OUR OWN
DEVILISH SHADOWS

in my years of failing
TO FIT IN THIS FOOLISH PUZZLE
I HAVE COME TO BELIEVE
THIS CHARMINGLY LUCKLESS,
UNFORTUNATE PLACE
EXISTS
ONLY TO ESCAPE FROM

and just like you and i
some stars align only once

IT'S ON THE LONG DRIVES HOME
WHEN THE SUN IS SETTING
OR WHEN I'M LYING STILL
IN A COLD BED
WHEN I MISS YOU THE MOST

WHEN ALL I WANT IS
YOUR HAND TO HOLD
OR ARMS TO WRAP AROUND ME

BUT NO MATTER HOW MANY STARS
I ASK TO BRING YOU BACK,
HOW MUCH I WISH FOR YOU
to be here
I KNOW IT IS NO LONGER
IN THE REALM OF POSSIBILITIES

AND AS I SIT ALONE
WITH THE MEMORY OF YOUR FINGERTIPS
TRACING ACROSS MY CHEST,

THE MOST PATHETIC PART IS
YOU WERE NEVER EVEN MINE
TO LOSE

I LEFT
you stayed behind
AND THAT'S A PROBLEM
WE DON'T KNOW HOW TO HANDLE

SO INSTEAD WE'LL FORGET
ABOUT EACH OTHER

BECAUSE THAT HURTS LESS
THAN HOLDING ON TO SOMEONE
WHO IS NO LONGER THERE

WHAT I'M MOST AFRAID OF
IS THAT ONE DAY
you will look at me
LIKE YOU LOOK AT A STRANGER—

WITH NO MORE LOVE
IN YOUR EYES

MAYBE IT WOULD BE BEST
TO JUST FORGET ABOUT ME—
about the way i made you feel

ABOUT THE MORNING I CRAWLED OUT
OF YOUR BED AND NEVER CAME BACK

ABOUT HOW I SHOULD'VE STAYED

JUST BECAUSE YOU NO LONGER

HEAR THE WORDS

i love you,

THAT DOESN'T MEAN

THEY ARE NOT

STILL

YOURS

THAT'S THE THING ABOUT THOSE
NECK DEEP IN SADNESS—
THEY DON'T WANT TO BE TOLD
THINGS WILL GET BETTER

NOT RIGHT NOW. NOT SO SOON.
YOUR WORLD IS STILL SPINNING
BUT LOOK AT THEM,
their world has stopped
THEY DON'T WANT TO BE TOLD
TIME WILL HEAL
AGAIN AND AGAIN AND AGAIN

ALL THEY WANT IS FOR YOU TO HEAR THEM
WITHOUT CONTRADICTING EVERY MOVE THEY MAKE

THEY WANT TO BE GENTLY UNDERSTOOD

THEY WANT TO BE ALLOWED TO HOLD THEIR GRIEF
FOR THE ONE THEY LOST, BECAUSE RIGHT NOW
THEY CAN'T MOVE ON. SO PLEASE DON'T ASK .
NOT YET.
RIGHT NOW, AS THEY STAND
MOTIONLESS IN THE CHAOS—
HEALING SOUNDS TOO MUCH LIKE FORGETTING

SOME DAYS I AM

MORE WILDFIRE

THAN WOMAN

THEY SAY ROMEO & JULIET ENDS IN TRAGEDY

BUT THINK ABOUT IT— THEY DIED,

but their love lives on

OUR LOVE DIED AND YET

WE MUST LIVE ON

THEIR SUFFERING IS OVER

AND OURS HAS JUST BEGUN

PLEASE, MY DARLING,
do not lose yourself
IN THE DEEP—

REMEMBER TO STAND
ON YOUR OWN TWO FEET
AND WITH YOUR HEAD
HELD HIGH,
LOVE YOURSELF FIRST

A PHOENIX LIKE ME
can only ever rise
AFTER I HAVE BEEN BURNT TO ASH

DO NOT BLAME ME FOR THE WORDS
THAT STIR INSIDE OF YOU—
for you have done the same to me

I AM CURSED WITH A THOUSAND THINGS
I NEED TO SAY AND NOT ENOUGH WORDS
BENEATH THE HEAVENS OR BEYOND
TO DO SO

ALL YOU WANTED WAS A DROP OF RAIN
BUT I GAVE YOU A HURRICANE

YOU TOLD ME NO MORE,
BUT DON'T YOU UNDERSTAND?

I CAN ONLY EVER LOVE
in the measure of oceans
OR NOT AT ALL

I'M SORRY
I CRUSHED YOUR HEART
IN MY HANDS—
all i was trying to do
WAS FEEL THE LOVE
I THOUGHT WAS THERE

IF YOU'RE GOING TO CHASE
AWAY YOUR DEMONS
YOU HAVE TO GO
to where they are

HE   LOOKS   AT   HER
LIKE   MOST   PEOPLE   LOOK
AT   GREAT   ART

HIS   EYES   TRACE   HER   FRAME
AS   HE   STANDS   IN   AWE
OF   HER   COLORS

HE   TRIES   TO   INTERPRET
WHAT   HE   SEES
BUT   HE'LL   NEVER   FULLY
U   N   D   E   R   S   T   A   N   D

QUICKLY   THOUGH
HE   MOVES   ON

BUT   SHE   WILL   LINGER
IN   HIS   MIND
FOR   QUITE   SOME   TIME

THERE   IS   NOTHING   ELSE
TO   BE   SAID

SHE   IS   A   MASTERPIECE
WITH   NO   ONE   LEFT
TO   LOVE   HER

I DON'T KNOW HOW TO TALK ABOUT YOU
WITHOUT FEELING LIKE
i lose you all over again
EVERY TIME THE STORY ENDS

SOME DAYS MORE THAN
OTHERS
I CAN FEEL IT
UNDER MY SKIN
AND AROUND MY BONES
the decay

IT'S HAPPENING EVEN NOW—
WE'RE DYING AS WE SPEAK

IT'S THE MOST BASIC LAW OF NATURE—
everything that lives must die
THIS ISN'T TO PUNISH US, NO,
QUITE THE OPPOSITE ACTUALLY

IT IS THIS CONSTANT CLOCK TICKING,
THIS NOTION THAT OUR DAYS ARE NUMBERED
THAT DRIVES US TO DO MORE, TO BE MORE
IN THE TIME THAT WE ARE GIVEN

OUR IMPENDING DEATHS,
OUR INESCAPABLE MORTALITY
IS WHAT GIVES LIFE ITS MEANING

IMAGINE, IF YOU WERE TO LIVE FOREVER,
HOW DULL ANOTHER SUNRISE WOULD BE

HOW TEDIOUS THE STARS
AND MUNDANE THE MOON

ETERNAL LIFE ON EARTH WOULD ULTIMATELY
STEAL THE HOPEFUL UNCERTAINTY
THAT MAKES US HUMAN,
AND THAT WOULD BE
THE MOST TRAGIC EXISTENCE
OF THEM ALL

I HAVE BEEN LOST FOR SO LONG
I FORGOT WHAT IT WAS LIKE
to be found

SUNDAY AFTERNOON, 2001

I VISITED MY GRANDMOTHER
EVERY SUNDAY AFTERNOON.
SHE LIVED BY HERSELF
IN A LITTLE HOUSE
DOWN THE ROAD FROM MINE.
OUR WHOLE FAMILY WOULD COME—
AUNTS, UNCLES, COUSINS.
SHE WOULD BE LAUGHING, USUALLY,
WHEN WE WALKED IN
AND HAVE LUNCH SET ON THE TABLE.
WE WOULD RUN OUT IN THE YARD
AND PLAY TAG OR CATCH BUTTERFLIES.
MY GRANDMOTHER WOULD WATCH FROM
THE PORCH AND SMOKE A CIGARETTE.
SHE'D BRING US POPSICLES WHEN
the summer heat set in.
WE WOULD REST AND SHE'D TELL ME
A STORY OF MY MOM AS A CHILD,
AND WHEN IT WAS TIME TO GO
SHE WOULD PICK ME UP IN HER ARMS
TO KISS MY CHEEK AND SAY GOODBYE.

SUNDAY AFTERNOON, 2017

I VISIT MY GRANDMOTHER
EVERY OTHER SUNDAY AFTERNOON, MAYBE LESS.
SHE LIVES WITH PATIENTS AND NURSES
IN AN ASSISTED LIVING HOME
FAR AWAY FROM MY HOUSE.
MY MOM AND SISTER COME— SOMETIMES MY DAD,
I DON'T REALLY SEE MY COUSINS ANYMORE.
WE FIND HER ASLEEP, USUALLY,
WHEN WE'RE LET IN
WITH A FEW CRACKERS ON HER SIDE TABLE.
SHE DOESN'T LEAVE THAT ROOM MUCH,
I DON'T THINK SHE'S BEEN OUTSIDE IN MONTHS.
SHE SLEEPS IN A HOSPITAL BED NOW
WITH AN OXYGEN TANK
AND OFTEN BRINGS UP HER PAIN.
her dementia has set in,
SHE WON'T REMEMBER WE CAME. THEY SAY SHE'S DYING
FROM LUNG CANCER AND ONLY HAS A FEW MONTHS.
SHE HAS A HARD TIME SITTING UP
SO I HAVE TO LEAN DOWN TO HUG HER
AND SHE KISSES MY CHEEK TO SAY GOODBYE.

SUNDAY AFTERNOON, 2019

I VISITED MY GRANDMOTHER TODAY
FOR THE FIRST SUNDAY AFTERNOON IN OVER A YEAR.
SHE'S BURIED NEXT TO MY PAPAW
IN THE CHURCH CEMETERY
NOT TOO FAR FROM MY HOUSE.
I CAME ALONE, THIS TIME—
BUT I AM STILL SURROUNDED BY FAMILY.
WE BRING HER FLOWERS, USUALLY,
WHEN WE STOP BY
AND LEAVE THEM ON HER GRAVE.
I SIT IN FRONT OF THE TOMBSTONE
AND WATCH LADYBUGS CRAWL ACROSS HER NAME.
I HOPE SHE'S HAPPY, WATCHING DOWN ON US,
WITH HEALTHY LUNGS, PLENTY OF ICE CREAM,
AND NO MORE PAIN.
the grief has set in
AND I DON'T REMEMBER WHAT IT WAS LIKE
WITHOUT IT.
WHEN IT WAS HER TIME TO GO,
I WASN'T THERE.
I NEVER EVEN SAID GOODBYE.

A DYING TREE STANDS TALL
IN A FOREST AMONGST THE LIVING.
HER BARE BRANCHES STILL SWAY
IN THE BREEZE, BUT CAN NO LONGER
GIVE SUPPORT WITHOUT BREAKING.

IT'S ONLY A MATTER OF TIME
BEFORE SHE FALLS TO THE GROUND.
ALL HER SEEDS HAVE GROWN ROOTS,
THERE'S NOTHING LEFT FOR HER TO DO
EXCEPT WATCH HER CHILDREN REACH
AWAY, CHOOSING THE BRIGHT
YOUNG SUNLIGHT OVER HER.

IT IS KNOWN BY NATURE'S LAWS,
SHE IS NO LONGER NEEDED.

SHE LAYS DOWN IN THE DIRT,
CRUSHING HER LIMBS,
SURROUNDED BY THE REMAINS
OF LOST LOVED ONES.

LOOKING UP, SHE SEES HER DAUGHTERS
standing taller than she ever could
AND AS THEIR RED LEAVES
COVER HER
SHE BEGINS TO ROT AWAY.

for my grandmother
1931 - 2018

IT'S IN HER EYES. ALL OF IT
A SHINING LIGHT OF THE UNIVERSE—
STARS THEMSELVES
INCOMPREHENSIBLE BEAUTY
OF ORDINARY THINGS

every hope of tomorrow
IS STORED BETWEEN HER EYELASHES
AND WHEN SHE LOOKS AT YOU,
YOU CAN'T HELP BUT BELIEVE
IN WONDERFUL THINGS TOO

SHE'S THE KIND OF GIRL
THAT CAN FIND THE BEAUTY
in anything

THROUGH HER BURNISHED BROWN EYES,
THE BROKEN BECOME MASTERPIECES AND
LOST THINGS ARE WORTHY

HER ARTIST'S SOUL LEADS AS
HER HONEST HEART FOLLOWS,
AND YOU MUST KNOW— ALTHOUGH
WHAT SHE WILL MAKE YOU FEEL MAY NOT
ALWAYS BE PRETTY & PERFECT, IT WILL
ALWAYS, ALWAYS BE REAL.

NEVERTHELESS, I CONTINUE TO HOPE
FOR THE DAY THAT I BELIEVE
SOMEONE IS DIFFERENT
AND THEY ACTUALLY TURN OUT TO BE
something more
THAN JUST ANOTHER DISAPPOINTMENT

I DON'T KNOW WHY
I SLEEP BEST WHEN HUGGING
MY PILLOW TO MY CHEST
AND STRETCHING MY LEG
OVER THE EMPTY SPACE
IN MY BED
but i think it has something
TO DO WITH YOU

I AM ALMOST ALWAYS CONTENT
BEING ON MY OWN

HOWEVER, FOR A MOMENT
IN THAT PLACE BETWEEN
WAKEFULNESS AND SLEEP
LONELINESS FLICKERS AS I LIE STILL
UNDER MY SHEETS

i become so very aware
OF THE EMPTINESS AROUND ME

I IMAGINE WHAT IT WOULD BE LIKE TO
FEEL HIS ARM PULLING ME
CLOSE TO HIS CHEST

HIS BREATH ON MY SKIN
HIS WARMTH ENGULFING ME
OUR HEARTS BEATING IN SYNC
MY MOST VULNERABLE SELF
SURRENDERED FOR HIS TAKING

OTHER THAN THAT, THOUGH,
I AM WELL ENOUGH ALONE

I WRITE YOUR NAME IN THE SAND
OVER AND OVER
BUT NO MATTER HOW MANY TIMES
I CARVE YOUR MEMORY IN

THE WAVES STILL COME
TO CRASH OVER MY SKIN
AND WASH AWAY THE LETTERS
INTO THE FORGOTTEN CORNERS
OF THE OCEAN

NEVER TO BE SEEN AGAIN

MY HANDS ARE ACHING

TO BE HELD AGAIN—

THE SPACES BETWEEN

MY FINGERS ARE LONELY,

THE PALM OF MY HAND

LONGS FOR WARMTH,

MY FINGERS CURL INTO

A FIST OVER AND OVER,

the empty air offers only solitude

AND I CAN FEEL IT IN MY BONES

THE WORLD AROUND ME CHANGED

ONCE I LOOKED PAST WHAT IT WAS

and began to see

WHAT IT COULD BE

YOU WERE NEVER LIKE THE OTHERS.
WITH THEM I COULDN'T SEE
PAST THE MOMENT,

BUT WITH YOU I COULD SEE
a million possibilities —

RELUCTANTLY WAKING UP
ON A COLD MORNING,
DIRTY CEREAL BOWLS, LOST KEYS,
FOUND KEYS, HOLDING HANDS
WHILE SHUFFLING THROUGH
CROWDED STREETS, GETTING LOCKED
OUT IN THE RAIN, WATCHING YOU
WATCH ME READ, SINGING TOO LOUDLY
IN THE CAR, ARGUING OVER MEANINGLESS
THINGS, FALLING ASLEEP
ON YOUR CHEST EVERY NIGHT

I LOOK AT YOU AND I SEE A LIFETIME

i have this terrible habit
of falling madly in love
with those who were never
meant to be mine

WE WERE LIKE TWO MATCHES
STRUCK TOGETHER,
TWICE AS BRIGHT AND
TWICE AS HOT,
but we burned out
TWICE AS FAST

r.clift

I KNOW SHE'S EVERYTHING
YOU WANT, BUT YOU CAN'T FALL
for a wild thing

TO GIRLS LIKE HER—
LOVE IS A CAGE

YOU MAY RUN ALONGSIDE HER, YES,
BUT SHE WILL NEVER BE YOURS

SHE WILL NEVER BELONG
TO ANYONE OTHER
THAN HERSELF

NOW I KEEP MY HEART
WHERE GOD INTENDED—
in a cage

WHEN I FOUND OUT I HAD
a spinning compass
WHERE A BEATING HEART
WAS MEANT TO BE

I REALIZED MY FIRST LOVE
WAS NEVER A PERSON—
BUT A PLACE

IN THE END WE WERE JUST

TWO BROKEN HEARTS

trying to remember

WHAT IT WAS LIKE TO BE WHOLE

I'M AFRAID TO ASK

if you're still in love with me

AND I THINK IT'S BECAUSE

I ALREADY KNOW THE ANSWER

THERE IS A WAR RAGING WITHIN YOU

A CONSTANT BATTLE BETWEEN

WHAT YOU KNOW

AND HOW YOU FEEL

IT MAY SEEM LIKE YOU'VE

surrendered yourself

TO THIS STRUGGLE INDEFINITELY

BUT ONCE YOU REALIZE

YOU CAN FIGHT

YOU REALIZE

YOU CAN WIN

THERE ARE DESIRES
THAT I'VE FILLED PAGES WITH,
SONNETS, LETTERS, POEMS—
OF LOVE, HAPPINESS, HEARTACHE, AND LOSS

THERE ARE A FEW I SWEAR
I COULD WRITE NOVELS ABOUT

AND THEN THERE'S YOU—
SOMEONE NOT EVEN WORTH A DROP OF INK

you will never be immortalized,
NOT IN MY WORDS.

YOU WILL BE ONLY WHAT YOU DESERVE—
FORGOTTEN

it only takes one
WRONG TOUCH
FROM AN UNINVITED PERSON
TO NEVER WANT TO BE TOUCHED
AGAIN

WHEN I DIE
IF YOU'RE GOING TO PUT ME IN THE GROUND
PLANT MY ASHES WITH A TREE
LET US GROW IN A FIELD OF OUR OWN
OUR BRANCHES REACHING FOR THE SKY
SO I CAN FEEL THE SUN'S WARMTH
ON MY FINGERTIPS

THE BIRDS WILL COME TO ME
FOR SAFETY AND COMFORT
CHILDREN WILL CLIMB MY ARMS
WITH ABUNDANT LAUGHTER
COUPLES WLL CARVE THEIR LOVE
INTO MY FLESH

AND I WILL WELCOME THEM ALL

I'LL BE THE BEACON
THAT DRAWS THEM IN
AND AS THE SOLE OASIS
OF THE VAST OPEN HILLSIDE

I, MYSELF, WILL BE VULNERABLE
FOR EVERYONE KNOWS, STANDING TALL
MAKES ONE MORE LIKELY
TO BE BURNED BY LIGHTNING
AND MAYBE THAT MEANS
I'LL DIE ALL OVER AGAIN

BUT AT LEAST THIS TIME
I WON'T BE ALONE

THE UNIVERSE GAVE ME

SOMEONE

BEAUTIFUL

WONDERFUL

PERFECT

and in love

WITH SOMEONE

ELSE

all my hands have
are each other
and that's not enough
to keep them warm

WHATEVER I TOUCH,
i seem to crumble
IN MY HANDS

SO PLEASE, MY DARLING,
DO NOT MAKE ME SWEEP UP THE DUST
OF ANOTHER UNSUSPECTING HEART

MAYBE THAT MEANS I STILL MISS YOU,
AND MAYBE THAT'S SOMETHING
YOU DON'T WANT TO HEAR—
BUT MAYBE,
you should get used to the idea
OF SOMEONE. SOMEWHERE. ALWAYS,
JUST A LITTLE,
MISSING YOU

SHY AWAY FROM SELFISHNESS AND GREED,
MY DEAR, TURN YOUR HEAD
CLOSE YOUR EYES

LISTEN TO THE BEAT
OF YOUR WARM HEART, INSTEAD

WITH EACH STEP YOU TAKE,
A THOUGHT CROSSES MY MIND—

WHAT DID I DO WRONG?
WHY DIDN'T YOU WANT ME?
AM I THE PROBLEM?
WHY WASN'T I ENOUGH?
WHAT'S WRONG WITH ME?
WILL A LOVE EVER STAY?
AND I HAVE TO PRETEND
LIKE I DON'T HEAR THEM
IN EVERY PAUSE

I HAVE TO PRETEND
THAT I'M NOT BREAKING
in every quiet moment of the day
EVERY TIME I AM LEFT ALONE
WITH MY THOUGHTS,
ALL I HEAR ARE FOOTSTEPS
AND THE SOUND
OF YOU WALKING AWAY

IT HAPPENED AGAIN—
I CLUTCH MY HEART AND CURSE
IT FOR THE DAMAGE IT HAS DONE AS
TEARS STAIN THE GROUND AROUND ME

I WATCH YOU WALK AWAY
GASPING FOR AIR
AND AS YOU HEAVE THROUGH
BURNED LUNGS

IT IS IN THIS MOMENT
WHEN YOU TRULY UNDERSTAND WHY
THEY ALL TRIED TO WARN YOU

I DON'T BLAME THEM ANYMORE
I'M A SUFFOCATOR, NOT A LOVER
AND I AM SO VERY AFRAID
THAT I WILL END UP
SMOTHERING
EVERY LAST PERSON THAT I CARE FOR

I WISH I COULD HAVE SAVED YOU,
FOUND A WAY TO LOVE YOU

but, my darling, i've tried
AND I JUST DON'T KNOW HOW

YOU GAVE ME WINGS
AND TOLD ME TO FLY
when all i wanted to do
WAS FALL ASLEEP
NEXT TO YOU

WE WERE TWO HEARTS
BEATING IN THE MOONLIGHT

TWO HEARTS BREAKING
AT DAWN

WHEN HE TOUCHED ME ALL I FELT
WAS THE GHOST OF YOU

nothing has felt brand new
SINCE YOU,
AND I THINK I WILL BE
CHASING THAT FEELING
FOR THE REST OF MY LIFE—

DESTINED TO BE SEARCHING
AND FOREVER UNSATISFIED

i wish i had a little more time
to fall in love with you

MY REMEMBRANCE OF YOU
IS ALL I HAVE LEFT—
BUT THIS ECHO WILL NEVER BE ENOUGH

FOR NO MATTER HOW OFTEN
I SHUT MY EYES TO SEE YOURS,
HOW CLOSELY I LISTEN
TO YOUR WORDS REPLAY
OVER AND OVER IN MY MIND,
OR HOW INTENTLY I CONJURE
THE GHOST OF YOUR ARMS
WRAPPING AROUND ME—

there is one irrefutable fact
POUNDING AGAINST MY HEART
THAT WILL NEVER CHANGE—
A MEMORY
CANNOT
LOVE ME BACK

r.clift

HOW CAN I POSSIBLY EXPLAIN THAT
I WAS JUST TOO AFRAID TO LOVE YOU

HOW CAN I POSSIBLY EXPLAIN THAT
I   STILL   DO

DON'T THINK OF YOUR HEART
AS LONELY, MY DARLING,
think of it as resting

ISN'T IT STRANGE
HOW TWO PEOPLE
or even two hundred

CAN SIT IN THE VERY SAME ROOM
WHILE ALL FEELING LONELY
AT THE SAME TIME?

SHE'S STILL WAVING

AT A PARADE

THAT HAS ALREADY

PASSED HER BY

THERE'S SOMETHING
ABOUT YOUR EYES
THAT MAKES ME NEVER WANT
to search for love
ANYWHERE ELSE

THERE'S A CERTAIN KIND OF GOODBYE
THAT HURTS MORE THAN THE REST

IT'S THE KIND OF GOODBYE YOU HEAR
FROM YOUR DYING GRANDMOTHER
OR FROM A LOVER LEAVING FOR GOOD,
SOMETIMES IT'S LESS DIRECT—
IT HIDES IN ALL THE OLD FRIENDS
THAT DRIFT AWAY AND BELOVED
MEMORIES THAT ARE TOO EASILY
FORGOTTEN

it's the final kind of goodbye —
ONE THAT DOESN'T
COME WITH A HELLO AGAIN

r.clift

MY NIGHTMARE IS IN THE WAKING—
IN THE THE REALIZATION
THAT YOU WERE NEVER HERE

THE FADING AWAY OF DELUSIONS
THAT DANCE THROUGH MY MIND
AND ENGULF ME
IN A FALSE SENSE OF EUPHORIA

IN A WORLD OF US, OF YOUR ARMS
WRAPPED AROUND ME,
YOUR VOICE ASKING ME TO STAY
all that never could be
NOT HERE. NOT IN THIS WORLD
BUT IN DRIFTING SLEEP, WHERE NOTHING QUITE
EXISTS IN THE WAY IT SHOULD

I CAN FEEL, VIVIDLY, AS IF IT WAS MEMORY—
HOW IT FEELS TO BE LOVED. TO BE WANTED

YOU ARE MINE & I AM YOURS
UNTIL THE MORNING COMES,
WHEN MY EYES BLINK INTO THE SUNLIGHT
AND I LOSE YOU ALL OVER AGAIN

I KNEW YOU WERE DIFFERENT
WHEN YOU TOOK MY BROKEN PIECES
AND HELD THEM IN YOUR HANDS,
AWESTRUCK— THE ONLY MAN I KNOW
WHO CAN POUR A PERFECT GIN RICKEY
AND FASHION THE SHARDS OF A SHATTERED GIRL
INTO A GLISTENING CHANDELIER
IN THE SAME NIGHT
look, YOU'D SAY, *you're light shines*
even brighter this way.
I NEVER KNEW FEARS COULD BE STRUNG
TOGETHER LIKE PEARLS UNTIL
YOU TOOK MINE AWAY ONE BY ONE
AND PLACED THEM GENTLY AROUND MY NECK
show them you're not afraid,
YOU'D SAY, *you've always been brave.*
NOW, ALTHOUGH WE MIGHT BE WORLDS APART,
I NEED YOU TO KNOW—
YOU'LL ALWAYS HAVE A HOME IN THIS HEART

TO THIS DAY, I CARRY ONLY ONE REGRET—
THAT NIGHT, UNDER THE LIGHTS,
I SHOULD HAVE DANCED WITH YOU INSTEAD

THE SOUND OF YOUR VOICE
MAKES ME BELIEVE
THAT MAYBE THIS HEART
still beats for a reason
AND MAYBE
I CAN FEEL SOMETHING
MORE
THAN NOTHING

you are everywhere i look
and nowhere to be found

YOU'RE THE ONE
THAT WALKED OUT OF MY LIFE
AND LOCKED THE DOOR,
so why
DO YOU KEEP ASKING FOR THE KEY?

I WANT TO BELIEVE THAT EVERYONE
I'VE EVER LOVED AND LOST WAS
WORTH IT,
WORTH THE HEARTACHE,
WORTH THE EMPTINESS
THEY LEAVE IN THEIR WAKE

I WANT TO BELIEVE THAT EVERYTHING
HAPPENS FOR A REASON
because without a reason,
what's the point?
BUT YOU—
US.
WE WERE BETTER OFF
AS STRANGERS

BE BOLD WITH YOUR HEART
AND TAKE RISKS DESPITE THE FEAR,
life doesn't pass without pain
SO WE MIGHT AS WELL PRETEND
WE HAVE CONTROL

SHE GIVES AWAY

LITTLE PIECES

OF HER HEART

LIKE CHARITY

AND DOESN'T KNOW

when to stop

I WILL PAINT YOUR SCARS INTO MASTERPIECES
AND CHIP AWAY AT YOUR BROKEN MARBLE HEART
UNTIL THE ANGEL WITHIN IS FREED

I WILL WHISPER POETRY IN YOUR EARS
AND SKETCH CHARCOAL MOUNTAINS
GENTLY ACROSS YOUR SKIN

I WILL PLUCK YOUR HEARTSTRINGS
LIKE A HARP SINGING
AND TEACH YOU HOW TO DANCE
WHILE HOLDING ME CLOSE

I WILL LOOK AT YOU AS IF YOU BELONG
IN A WORLD-RENOWNED MUSEUM
AND I WILL VIEW EVERY IMPERFECTION
AS PRICELESS

i will love you
IN THE ONLY WAY AN ARTIST CAN—
WITH EVERYTHING I AM

THERE IS A KIND OF MAGIC WITHIN HER

THAT EVEN THE MOST ANCIENT

HAVE NEVER FULLY UNDERSTOOD,

PASSED THROUGH GENERATIONS

OF WILD, WILLFUL, WONDROUS WOMEN—

AND THIS, WHETHER SHE BELIEVES IT OR NOT,

begs the conclusion

THAT THE UNIVERSE CAN ONLY EVER

BE COMPLETE WITH HER IN IT

IF THERE IS MAGIC IN THIS WORLD
IT IS NOT IN ONLY YOU OR ME,
but the space in between
AND THE LOVE THAT LIVES THERE

THE MOON MUST BE SO JEALOUS
OF THE CLOSENESS
OF THE STARS
THE INSEPARABLE CONSTELLATIONS
SURROUNDING HER

I SUPPOSE THIS IS WHY
SHE TRIES TO PULL THE SEA CLOSER
EACH NIGHT
but even in her endless efforts
HE WILL ALWAYS BE
JUST OUT OF REACH

I PITY HER LONELINESS IN SPACE
FOR SHE AND I ARE THE SAME

you are so much more
than the darkness
that surrounds you

A SHOOTING STAR IS SEEN AS
RARE AND EXTRAORDINARY
WHEN IN REALITY
IT'S CRASHING TO ITS DEATH

I IMAGINE HOW IT MUST BE
SUFFERING
BURNING ALIVE
AS IT'S THROWN
FROM THE ONLY HOME
IT HAS EVER KNOWN

while there you stand
SELFISHLY IN AWE
MAKING A WISH UPON
ITS FATAL FALL

WHEN I WAS LITTLE

I USED TO DREAM WITH MY EYES OPEN—

LEAVING MY WINDOW CRACKED EVERY NIGHT

JUST IN CASE

A BOY WHO LOST HIS SHADOW MIGHT BE

SEARCHING FOR SOMEONE TO TAKE AWAY,

PAST THE STARS, ACROSS THE UNIVERSE

TO A LAND OF GREAT ADVENTURE

BUT HE NEVER CAME

my room turned cold

AND ALL I HAD LEFT TO DO

WAS TO CLOSE MY EYES AND

GROW UP

r.clift

SHE HOLDS THE INTIMATE WARMTH
OF SUMMER UNDERNEATH HER SKIN
AND EXHALES WITH THE
NERVOUS UNDERSTANDING
that she has something to lose

AROUND HER NECK—
A DEAR TOKEN OF HIS
TO REMIND HER
THAT THE KIND OF LOVE
SHE'S READ ABOUT IN BOOKS
IS STILL WORTH FIGHTING FOR

YOU AND I MUST HAVE BEEN A DREAM,
only ever meant to exist
IN ANOTHER WORLD FAR FROM THIS ONE—
WHERE SOMETHING
EVEN AS IMPOSSIBLE
AS LOVE
COULD BE OURS

SADNESS IS LIKE THE RAIN—
BUT IT'S ALWAYS LIKE THE RAIN

WHY CAN'T SADNESS BE PRETTY
LIKE SUNSETS AND FIREFLIES?

IMAGINE THIS—
THE WOE OF HUMANITY CAPTURED
IN GLASS JARS AS ORANGE RAYS DIM
INTO AN INDIGO EVENING

ON OUR KITCHEN SHELVES
WE KEEP OUR HEARTACHE, GRIEF, AND SORROW
ENCASED WITH PUNCTURED LIDS
so they can breathe
EACH SHINING
WITH A GENTLE GLOW,
ALL NIGHT,
UNTIL THE SUN RISES AGAIN
AND ALL THE SUFFERING
WE'VE COLLECTED
IS RELEASED INTO MORNING—

AND AS TINY DROPLETS
FALL FROM THE SKY
WE SMILE

MY DARLING, PLEASE

DO NOT FEEL SO ASHAMED

OF YOUR SCARS

they were only ever trying

TO HEAL YOU

THERE ARE TIMES WHEN

REMINISCENCE

SWALLOWS ME WHOLE

AND I CANNOT DISMISS

all the serendipities

THAT HAVE SLIPPED

THROUGH MY FINGERS

MY DEAR, YOU GO ON ABOUT HOW
YOU WISH TO SEE THE WORLD
BUT DON'T YOU KNOW—
EVERY OCEAN WOULD BE LUCKY
TO BE TOUCHED BY YOU

THE SUN RISES FOR YOU TO FEEL
ITS WARMTH AND THE WIND BLOWS
TO PLAY WITH YOUR HAIR

EVERY CITY EAGERLY ANTICIPATES
YOUR ARRIVAL AND EACH MOUNTAIN
WAITS FOR YOU TO CLIMB IT

the earth has heard whispers of you
AND YOUR TRAVELER'S SOUL

IT IS NOT ONLY YOU
THAT LONGS TO SEE THE WORLD,

THE WORLD LONGS TO SEE YOU

WHEN DID THIS PLAGUING THOUGHT THAT I WAS MADE
TO BE ALONE BECOME SUCH AN INTEGRAL PART OF ME?
WHERE DID IT FIRST COME FROM?
WHO GAVE IT TO ME?
WHO MADE ME FEEL SO UNWANTED
THAT I BRAND MYSELF SO?

I REMEMBER A TIME WHEN I WAS FEARLESS, CARE-FREE,
I USED TO STAND TALL WITHOUT HAVING TO THINK ABOUT IT

I USED TO BELIEVE IN TRUE LOVE AND HAPPILY EVER AFTERS
WHERE DID SHE GO? WHERE DID THAT LITTLE GIRL GO?
THE ONE THAT NEVER WANTED TO GROW UP

THE ONE THAT LEFT HER WINDOW CRACKED AT NIGHT
FOR A CHANCE AT FINDING NEVERLAND

THE ONE THAT LOOKED AT A BROKEN MAN
AND SAW AN ANGEL

where did she go?
I STILL REMEMBER HER

AS LONG AS I REMEMBER HER, SHE IS A PART OF ME—
AND AS LONG AS SHE IS A PART OF ME,
I HAVE TO BELIEVE I CAN FIND HER AGAIN

r.clift

I ONCE MET A BUTTERYFLY WITH TORN WINGS—
THEY WERE A BRILLIANT BLUE,
LIKE NIGHT–VELVET SKY
WITH LITTLE WHITE DOTS
SPACED APART IN CONSTELLATIONS

I TOLD HER THAT HER WINGS WERE BEAUTIFUL,
BUT SHE DIDN'T BELIEVE ME

SHE FLAPPED AND FLAPPED,
ONLY STIRRING THE AIR AROUND HER
NEVER ABLE TO LIFT FOR LONG ABOVE THE DIRT
BEFORE CRASHING DOWN AGAIN

she's a broken thing now,
AND THERE'S NOTHING I CAN DO
TO HELP HER

HOW AM I SUPPOSED TO TELL A CREATURE
MADE TO SOAR THROUGH THE CLOUDS
THAT SHE MUST LIVE THE REST OF HER LIFE
ON THE GROUND?

HE KISSED ME AS IF HE WAS DROWNING
AND I WAS THE AIR HE NEEDED
TO SURVIVE

it was at that moment
THAT I REALIZED EVERY OTHER KISS
I'VE EVER HAD IN MY LIFE
HAD BEEN WRONG

THERE IS A HIGH PRICE TO PAY ON A NOMADIC SOUL—
YOU WILL NEVER FEEL COMPLETELY AT HOME AGAIN
AS YOU LEAVE PIECES OF YOURSELF BEHIND
EVERYWHERE YOU GO

YOUR RESTLESSNESS WILL RULE YOU
FOR THE REST OF YOUR LIFE
AND YOU WILL WEAR OUT THE WORD
GOODBYE

YOU WILL NEVER BE THE SAME PERSON
TWO DAYS IN A ROW—
CHANGE WILL BE YOUR ONLY CONSTANT

YOU WILL JOURNEY TO SEE BEAUTY AND TRAGEDY
AND YOU WILL BE FILLED WITH MORE QUESTIONS
THAN ANSWERS

SOME DAYS IT WILL HURT
it may even break your heart

BUT THIS PRICE IS NOTHING
COMPARED TO THE RICHNESS YOU WILL FIND
IN LOVING AND KNOWING THIS EARTH
FROM MORE THAN ONE PLACE

r.clift

NO MATTER HOW A HEART IS TORN,
SAVAGED, ABUSED, OR SCARRED,

it will beat on
STEADILY
UNTIL ITS VERY LAST DAY

WHEN ALL ITS LOVE HAS BEEN DRAINED
AND ALL ITS PAIN FORGIVEN

WITH EVERY BREATH YOU TAKE

EVERY MINUTE THAT PASSES

YOU ARE LIVING AND YOU ARE DYING—

REMEMBER BOTH

DEAR YOU,

Yes you, whoever is feeling these words.
You have been carrying those books for so long, you don't
even know how to put them down.
you don't want to, you can't. i know.

Listen for a moment, it's supposed to be scary,
you've been writing memories in those pages for
years and years and years and in that time
you have never had to write without them—
but things have changed. They're gone
and no matter how long you hold those memories
to your chest, no matter how tight, it will never be
how it used to be.

Don't think of it as putting those books down in a way
that means you must forget everything in them—
forget all that you ever had, all that you thought
would last forever— because those books—
that time in your life is still a part of you.
It will always be a part of you, but you cannot keep holding
on to something that is already gone.
Your arms are tired, you are so tired, I know,
so put those memories on a shelf & love them,
cherish them, the good and the bad.
but leave them.

YOU, MY LOVE, ARE STILL A GREAT WRITER,
and there is ink in your pen for a reason.
This blank page looks initimidating now, it seems impossible
to write on your own, but you can. You must.

For your life, your purpose, is not lost, this one chapter is simply ending.
It is time to write a new narrative— one of healing, of strength
coming back, because believe me when I say some of the best days
of your life haven't even happened yet.

Keep that blank page close, write today, live today,
because life is happening now and every single tragic, beautiful
wonderful, unpredictable, ordinarily extraordinary moment
of your existence, from this second onwards is

MEANT TO BE REMEMBERED.

— r.clift

ACKNOWLEDGEMENTS

THIS JOURNEY HAS NOT BEEN SIMPLE — AT TIMES I FELT AS THOUGH
MAYBE, I WAS ON THE WRONG PATH. CHASING FOOLISH DREAMS.
I ESPECIALLY FELT THIS WAY WHILE DROWNING IN GRIEF.
IT CAN BE HARD TO SEE CLEARLY, THAT'S WHY I AM SO INCREDIBLY
THANKFUL FOR THE PEOPLE WHO HAVE STAYED BY MY SIDE.
WHO HOLD MY HAND AND TELL ME TO KEEP GOING.
HERE, I AIM TO THANK YOU — THOUGH IN TRUTH,
WORDS WILL NEVER BE ENOUGH.

THANK YOU to my family: my mother, my father, my
grandparents, my sister, Laura. You have taught me how to
hold my own grief and how to do so with enduring love.

THANK YOU to my dearest friends, my sisters— Lauren,
Sarah, Olivia, Carley, and Vanessa for carrying me through
the hard days & for being there every step of the way.

THANK YOU to Emily and Ellen, for becoming an integral
part of this collection and trusting in me to bring
this art to life.

THANK YOU to the poetry community, for listening to my
words and for investing your time and heart into my work.

THANK YOU to my late professor, Arthur Smith, who
gave me poetry and taught me that truly living
is the most important thing one can do.
"The inspiration is the best part of the poem
and you had nothing to do with it."

travel photo Locations

ABOUT THE *poet*

Rachel Clift is a writer and photographer based in
the mountains of East Tennessee.
More than anything, she longs to inspire people–
in some way, somehow, to love who they are and
live life courageously.
Bursting at the seams with dreams of flying again, it's only
a matter of time before she takes off to experience even
more of the world.
She is a firm believer that traveling with only a backpack
and little to no plans is the most marvelous thing one can
do and no matter how many times a heart may break–
it will always keep beating.

Thank you, my darling, for reading –
for giving these aching words a home.
Please remember to be patient with your heart,
choose courage when you can, and above all

BE KIND

♡ xx *Rachel*

FOLLOW THE EVER-CHANGING JOURNEY

@R.CLIFTPOETRY ON INSTAGRAM

Write your own poem here,
take a photo when you're done,
and send it to me.

{R.CLIFTPOETRY ON INSTAGRAM}

i would love to read your words.

xx Rachel

· ·

Lightning Source UK Ltd.
Milton Keynes UK
UKHW020809151021
392249UK00007B/258